MYSTICAL
ASTROLOGY
ACCORDING TO
IBN 'ARABI

The Fons Vitae Titus Burckhardt Series

Fons Vitae is dedicated to preserving in print for future generations the extraordinarily important and timeless work of Titus Burckhardt, who devoted his life to the exposition of Universal Truth, that wisdom "uncreate" in the realm of metaphysics, cosmology, and sacred art. In addition to Burckhardt's *Alchemy: Science of the Cosmos, Science of the Soul, Letters of a Sufi Master,* and *Moorish Culture in Spain,* Fons Vitae is honored to add to the series *Sacred Art in East and West, Mirror of the Intellect,* and *Mystical Astrology According to Ibn 'Arabi.*

An eminent Swiss metaphysician and scholar of oriental languages Titus Burckhardt (1908- 1984) devoted his life to the timeless and universal wisdom present in Sufism, Vedanta, Taoism, Platonism, and the other great esoteric and sapiential traditions. Though an art historian like his great uncle the renowned Jacob Burckhardt, his main interest was the spiritual use and meaning to be found in Eastern and Western art and architecture, and the expression of the sacred in the lives of saints.

Fons Vitae is grateful to the Chester Beatty Library in Dublin for permission to include illustrations from the 16th century Persian manuscript *Suwar al-Kawakib of al-Sufi* or *The Shape of the Stars.* Written by the Persian astronomer, Abd al-Rahman al-Sufi, in about AD 960, this astronomical treatise is based ultimately on an ancient Greek source, Ptolemy's *Almagest.* A masterpiece of observational astronomy, its illustrations of the constellations are Muslim reinterpretations of the original Greek models.

Mystical Astrology According to Ibn 'Arabi

TITUS BURCKHARDT

Translated from French by
Bulent Rauf

FONS VITAE

Previously published as
*Une Clef Spirituelle de L'Astrologie Musulmane
d'après Mohyi-d-din Ibn 'Arabi*
Les Editions Traditionelles, Paris, 1950
and as
*Clé Spirituelle de L'Astrologie Musulmane
d'après Mohyiddin Ibn 'Arabi*
Archè, Milan, 1974.

First English translation by
Beshara Publications, Abingdon, England, 1977

This new, illustrated edition published by
Fons Vitae
49 Mockingbird Valley Drive
Louisville, KY 40207
www.fonsvitae.com
© 2001

Printed in Canada

ISBN: 1-887752-43-9

Library of Congress Control Number: 2001094850

Foreword

As the term astrology means the practical application of astronomy to human use our response to it must necessarily hinge on our understanding of what it means to be human.

What is that 'favourable moment' which the Buddha urges us to grasp? Why does he congratulate those who 'have seized their moment' and lament those 'for whom the moment is passed'?[1] The explanation lies in the traditional[2] view of time. Illumination, or the goal of human existence, is instantaneous in relation to the long cosmic journey of passing time. It is a comprehension of Reality which comes 'in a flash' like lightning. This favourable moment or paradoxical instant suspends duration and places the recipient into a timeless present. This timeless present is paradoxical in as much as it is qualitatively different from that illusive 'profane' present that barely exists between two non-entities, the past and the future, and apparently ceases with our death. Neither does the 'profane' experience have any bearing on the prolongation, beyond time, that the 'favourable moment' brings, which can be likened to a glance 'outside' time.

For those of us who have been educated in the 'values' of modern Western industrial culture the traditional view of time is as difficult to grasp as is its unfoldment represented by the traditional symbolism of astrology.

[1] *Khanātitā; Samyuta Nikāya,* IV 126.
[2] Tradition in our present usage means the animating principle of a normal society or the 'presiding idea' which underlies and inspires the whole life of a people.

For the serious investigator, who is determined to get to the roots of traditional principles this small book is a gold-mine. It is specificaly drawn from the perspective of the Islamic contemplative tradition, committed to written form by Muhyiddin Ibn 'Arabi, and unfolds the timeless spectrum of the orders of being as they relate to time and space in 'our' world.

In this volume Titus Burckhardt has distilled the essential symbolism underlying spiritual astrology – as in contradistinction to divinatory astrology: '... for the individual curiosity, all "oracle" remains equivocal and may even reinforce ... error ...' As, '... man cannot remove the veil of his ignorance except by or through something which transcends his individual will.' In doing so he points with great clarity to the fundamental difference between this traditional viewpoint and the 'individualist' and 'historicist' viewpoint which contemporary Western opinion has inherited from the flood-tide of Aristotelianism, which invaded the Middle Ages and has dominated its world feeling ever since. So much so that few contemporary Western thinkers would even know of, let alone take into consideration, the principle, so fundamental to the tradition represented by Plato, as that of Perichoresis. This process, or 'permeation of the divine presence', arises from the 'platonic' teaching that states that the world of materiality is unequivocally dependent for its being and existence on the principal first cause, and as such is merely its furthest reflexion or exteriorised expression. As light both causes and permeates shadow, so the divine presence permeates, through perichoresis, to the heart of all materiality. Aristotelianism asserts that universals only have existence in so far as they characterize individual concrete things – thereby implying that universals only exist in the human mind that 'abstracts' them from 'things'. This inversion of the teaching of Plato's academy (that Aristotle left) gave rise to the eventual divorce of mind from matter and spirit from body and soul due to the irreconcilability of individual 'thingness' with the traditional doctrine of the total permeability or effusion of the divine presence recognisable as the Universals.

It is no mere chance that Ibn 'Arabi was surnamed 'Son of Plato' (Ibn Aflatun) because of this fundamental viewpoint within the revelation of Islam, that asserts the dependence of the sensible world on the intelligible world, and the intelligible in return on the ontological principle of Unity. To understand the starting point of this perspective of spiritual astrology one needs to make a definitive effort of reorientation; for we 'moderns' are almost unknowingly educated in the totalitarian philosophical empiricism of Aristotelianism.

The reward for the effort may not only open some very valuable doors onto the real significance of astrology in the traditional sense but those same doors may well lead out of the prison of 'historicism' to that 'favourable moment' where, as an integral person, we neither deny ourselves our own historic moment, nor consent to be solely identified with it.

KEITH CRITCHLOW

I

THE WRITTEN work of the 'greatest Master' (ash-shaikh al-akbar) Sufi, Muhyiddin Ibn 'Arabi, contains certain considerations on astrology which permit one to perceive how this science, which arrived in the modern occident only in a fragmentary form and reduced only to some of its most contingent applications, could be related to metaphysical principles, thereby relating to a knowledge self-sufficient in itself. Astrology, as it was spread through the Middle Ages within Christian and Islamic civilizations and which still subsists in certain Arab countries, owes its form to the Alexandrine hermeticism; it is therefore neither Islamic nor Christian in its essence; it could not in any case find a place in the religious perspective of monotheistic traditions, given that this perspective insists on the responsibility of the individual before its Creator and avoids, by this fact, all that could veil this relationship by considerations of intermediary causes. If, all the same, it were possible to integrate astrology into the Christian and Moslem esotericism, it is because it perpetuated, vehicled by hermeticism, certain aspects of a very primordial symbolism: the contemplative penetration of cosmic atmosphere, and the identification of spontaneous appearances – constant and rhythmic – of the sensible world with the eternal prototypes corresponding in fact to a mentality as yet primitive, in the proper and positive sense of this term. This implicit primordiality of the astrological symbolism flares up in contact with spirituality, direct and univer-

9

sal, of a living esotericism, just like the scintillation of a precious stone flares up when it is exposed to the rays of light.

Muhyiddin Ibn 'Arabi encloses the facts of the hermetic astrology in the edifice of his cosmology, which ·he summarises by means of a schemata of concentric spheres by taking, as the starting point and as terms of comparison, the geocentric system of the planetary world as the Medieval world conceived it. The 'subjective' polarisation of this system – we mean by that the fact that the terrestrial position of the human being serving as the fixed point to which will be related all the movements of the stars – here symbolises the central role of man in the cosmic whole, of which man is like the goal and the centre of gravity. This symbolic perspective naturally does not depend upon the purely physical or spatial reality, the only one envisaged by modern astronomy, of the world of the stars; the geocentric system, being in conformity with the reality as it presents itself immediately to the human eyes, contains in itself all the logical coherence requisite to a body of knowledge for constituting an exact science. The discovery of the heliocentric system, which corresponds to a development both possible and homogeneous but very particular to the empirical knowledge of the sensible world, obviously could not prove anything against the central cognition of the human being in the cosmos; only, the possibility of conceiving the planetary world as if one were contemplating it from the non-human position, and even as if one could make abstraction of the existence of the human being – even though its consciousness still remains the 'container' of all conceptions – had produced an intellectual dis-equilibrium which shows clearly that the 'artificial' extension of the empirical knowledge has in it something of the abnormal, and that it is, intellectually, not only indifferent but even detrimental.[1]

[1] ". . . The 'scientific errors' due to a collective subjectivity – for example that of the human kind and the terrestrial beings in general seeing the sun revolving around the earth – translate as true symbolism, and consequently 'truths', which are obviously independent of the simple facts which carry

The discovery of heliocentricism has had effects resembling certain vulgarisations of esotericism; we are here thinking above all of those inversions of point of view which are proper to esoteric speculation;[2] the confrontation of respective symbolisms of geocentric and heliocentric systems shows very well what such an inversion is : in fact, the fact that the sun, source of the light of the planets is equally the pole which rules their movements, contains, like all existent things, an evident symbolism and represents in reality, always from a symbolic and

---

them in an altogether provisional manner; the subjective experience, like the one we have just mentioned as an example, has obviously nothing of the fortuitous. It is 'legitimate' for man to admit that the earth is flat, because empirically it is; on the other hand it is completely useless to know that it is round since this knowledge adds nothing to the symbolism of appearances, but destroys it uselessly and replaces it by another which could never express the same reality, all the while posing the inconvenience of being contrary to the immediate and general human experience. The knowledge of facts for themselves do not have, outside the interested scientific applications, any value; in other words one is either situated in the absolute reality, and in that case the facts are no longer anything, or one is situated in the domain of facts, and then in any case in ignorance. Aside from that, one must say again that the destruction of the natural and immediate symbolism of facts – such as the flat form of the earth or the circular movement of the sun – brings about serious inconvenience for the civilisation wherein they are produced, which is fully demonstrated by the example of the occidental civilizations."
(Frithjof Schuon; 'Fatalité et Progrès', in *Etudes Traditionelles*.)

[2] There are indices that allow one to suppose that the Pythagoricians already knew of the heliocentric system. It is not excluded that this knowledge was always maintained, and that the discovery of Copernicus is in reality nothing other than a simple vulgarisation, like so many other 'discoveries' of the Renaissance.

Copernicus himself refers, in his preface – addressed to Pope Paul III – to his fundamental book, *On the Orbits of the Celestial Bodies*, to Hicetas of Syracuse and to certain citations of Plutarch. Hicetas was a Pythagorician; and Aristotle, in his book, *Of the Sky*, says that "The Italic philosophers, who are called Pythagoricians, are of a contrary opinion to most other physicians, because they affirm that the centre of the world is occupied by the fire, whereas the earth, which is a star, moves in a circle around this centre, thus causing day and night." Aristarcus of Samos, astronomer in Alexandria about 250 BC, taught equally the heliocentric system; in the same way Al-Birûnî, the famous Moslem compiler of Hindu traditions, recounts that certain Indian sages hold that the earth turns around the sun.

spiritual point of view, a complementary point of view to that of the geocentric astronomy.[3]

Muhyiddin Ibn 'Arabi englobes in a certain fashion the essential reality of heliocentricism in his cosmological edifice: like Ptolemy and like those all through the Middle Ages he assigns to the sun, which he compares to the 'Pole' (*qutb*) and to the 'heart of the world' (*qalb al-'âlam*), a central position in the hierarchy of the celestial spheres, and this by assigning equal numbers of superior skies and inferior skies to the sky of the sun; he amplifies nevertheless the system of Ptolemy by yet again underlining the symmetry of the spheres with respect to the sun: according to his cosmological system, which he probably holds from the Andalusian Sufi Ibn Masarrah, the sun is not only in the centre of the six known planets – Mars (*al-mirikh*), Jupiter (*al-mushtarî*) and Saturn (*az-zuhal*) being further away from the Earth (*al-ardh*) than the Sun (*ash-shams*), and Venus (*az-zuhrah*), Mercury (*al-utarid*) and the Moon (*al-qamar*) being closer – but beyond the sky of Saturn is situated the vault of the sky of the fixed stars (*falak al-kawâkib*), that of the sky without stars (*al-falak al-atlas*), and the two supreme spheres of the 'Divine Pedestal' (*al-kursî*) and of the 'Divine Throne' (*al-'arsh*), concentric spheres to which symetrically correspond the four sub-lunar spheres of ether (*al-athîr*), of air (*al-hawâ*), of water (*al-mâ*) and of earth (*al-ardh*). Thus is apportioned seven degrees to either side of the sphere of the sun, the Divine (Throne) symbolising the synthesis of all the cosmos, and the centre of the earth being thereof both the inferior conclusion and the centre of fixation.

[3] That which renders irreconcilable the two systems is obviously not their 'optic' side, but the theory on gravitation related to the heliocentric system.

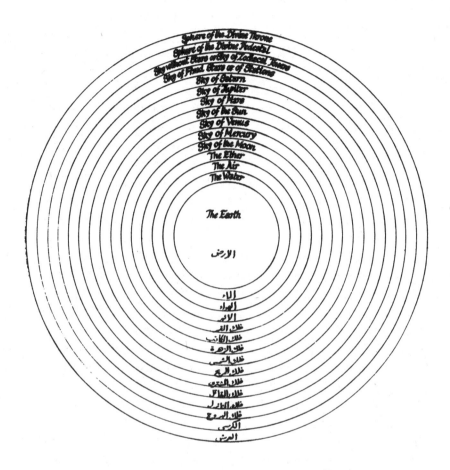

It goes without saying, that among all the spheres of this hierarchy, only the planetary spheres and those of the fixed stars correspond as such to the sensible experience, even though they should not be envisaged only within this relationship; as to the sub-lunary spheres of ether – which do not signify here the quintessence, but the cosmic centre in which the fire is re-absorbed – of air and of water, one should rather see a theoretical hierarchy according to the degrees of density, rather than spatial spheres. As for the supreme spheres of the 'Divine Pedestal' and the 'Throne' – the former containing the skies and the earth, and the latter englobing all things[4] – their spherical form is purely symbolic, and they mark the passage from astronomy to metaphysical and integral cosmology :[5] the sky without Stars (al-falak al-atlas), which is a 'void', and which because of this fact is no more spatial, but rather marks the 'end' of space, also marks by that the discontinuity between the formal and informal; in fact this appears like a 'nothingness' from the formal point of view, whereas the principial appears like a 'nothingness' from the point of view of the manifested. One would have understood that this passing from the astronomic point of view to the cosmological and metaphysical point of view has in it nothing of the arbitrary: the distinction between the visible sky and a sky avoiding our view is real, even if its application is nothing but symbolic, and the 'invisible' here spontaneously becomes the 'transcendent', in conformity with Oriental symbolism; the spheres of informal manifestation – the 'Throne' and the 'Pedestal' – are expressly called the 'invisible world' ('âlam al-ghaïb), the word ghaïb meaning all that is beyond the reach of our vision, which shows this symbolic correspondence between the 'invisible' and the 'transcendent'.

The 'Pedestal', on which are placed the 'feet' of the One who is sitting on the 'Throne', represents the first 'polarisation', or distinctive determination with respect to formal manifestation – determination which comprises an 'affirmation' and a 'negation' to which correspond, in the Revealed Book, the Commandment (al-amr) and the Prohibition (an-nahî).

[4] As the Koran teaches. According to an expression of the Prophet the world is contained in the 'Divine Pedestal' and this itself is contained in the 'Throne' like a ring in an earth mould.

[5] In certain symbolic schemata of Sheikh al-akbar, one finds other spheres larger than that of the 'Throne', this symbolism naturally being susceptible of an extension more or less great; meanwhile the hierarchy that we have just enumerated represents in itself a complete whole, because the 'Divine Throne' englobes all manifestation. This is what Muhyiddin Ibn 'Arabi teaches, in conformity to the Koran, in the 'Revelations of Mecca' al-futuhat al-makkiyah); in other writings he will speak of a whole hierarchy of different 'Thrones' which constitute the principal degrees of informal Existence.

The sky without stars (*al-falak al-atlas*) is also the sky of the twelve 'towers' (*burûj*) or 'signs' of the zodiac; and these are not identical with the 12 zodiacal constellations contained in the sky of the fixed stars (*falak al-kawâkib* or *falak al-manâzil*), but represent 'virtual determinations' (*maqâdir*) of the celestial space and are not differentiated except by their relationship to planetary 'stations' or 'mansions' (*manâzil*) projected on the sky of the fixed stars. Here there is a very important point for the understanding of Arab and occidental astrology; we shall return to it later on.

The traditional cosmology does not make an explicit differentiation between the planetary skies in their corporal and visible reality, and that which corresponds to them in the subtle order; because the symbol is essentially identified with the thing it symbolises, and there is no reason for making a distinction between the one and the other, except where this distinction can be made practically, and finally that the derived aspect can be taken separately for the whole, as happens when the corporal form of a living being is taken for the whole being; whereas in the case of the planetary rhythms – because it is these that constitute the different 'skies' – this distinction cannot be made except by the theoretical application of mechanical conceptions which are foreign to the contemplative mentality of traditional civilisations.[6]

The planetary spheres are therefore at the same time part of the corporal world, and degrees of the subtle world; the Sky without stars, which is the extreme limit of the sensible world, symbolically envelopes all human states including all the superior 'prolongations' of this state; the *Sheikh al-akbar* in fact situates the paradisiac states between the sky of fixed stars

[6] Thus the Indians of N. America who hold no theories on electricty, can see in the lightning the power itself of the 'Lightning Bird', which is the Divine Spirit in macrocosmic manifestation : there are even cases where the percussion of the lightning gives spiritual powers, which would not be possible for Europeans who are in the habit of mentally separating sensible forms from their 'supernatural' archetypes.

and the sky without stars – or the sky of the zodiacal 'Towers' – the superior paradises touching so to speak upon the informal existence, though remaining circumscribed by the subtle form of the human being. The sky of the zodiacal 'towers' therefore, with respect to the integral human state, is the 'place' of the archetypes.[7]

That which is situated beyond the skies of the fixed stars, between this latter and the skies without stars is maintained in pure duration, whereas that which is below the sky of the fixed stars is subjected to generation and corruption. It may seem that the sphere of the supreme sky, which is the *primum mobile*, is identified with the incorruptible world, whereas movement evolves necessarily in time. But that which one must remember here is that the revolution of the most vast sky, being itself the fundamental measure of time according to which all other movement is measured, cannot itself be susceptible to temporal measure, which corresponds to the indifferentiation of pure duration. Just as the concentric movements of the stars are differentiated within the order of their successive dependance, in the same way the temporal condition becomes precise, or contracts in some way, according to the measure where it interferes with the spatial condition; and by analogy, the different spheres of the planetary worlds – or more exactly the rhythms of their revolutions – graduating starting with the indefinable limits of this space until the terrestrial centre, can be considered as so many successive degrees of the temporal 'contraction'.[8]

[7] It has to do with the cosmological definition of the paradisiac states, and not with their implicit symbolism which makes it that their descriptions can be transposed to the highest degrees of existence and even to the pure Being, since one speaks, in sufic language, of the 'paradise of the Essence' (*djannat adh-dhât*).

[8] For this reason, the astrological hierarchy of the planetary sky situates Mercury between Venus and the Earth since Mercury moves more rapidly than Venus, and this in spite of the fact that Venus is closer to the Earth, and Mercury closer to the Sun.

II

ASTROLOGICAL SYMBOLISM resides in 'points of junction' of the fundamental conditions of the sensible world, and especially in the junctions of time, space and number. We know that the definition of the regions or parts of the great sphere of the sky without stars by means of reference points that the fixed stars offer coincide in astronomy, with the definition of divisions of time. Now, the limit-sphere of the sky is not measurable except by reason of the directions of the space; when one speaks of parts of the sky one does no other than define the directions; on the other hand, these are the expressions of the qualitative nature of the space, so that the limits of the spatial indefinity are reintegrated in some ways in the qualitative aspect in question, the whole of the directions that radiate from one centre virtually containing all the possible spatial determinations.[1] The extreme and indefinite expansion of these directions is the vault of the sky without stars and their centre is each living being which is on earth, without the 'perspective' of the directions changing from one individual to the other, because our visual axes coincide without confusion when we fix our gaze on one point of the celestial vault – in which is expressed obviously a coincidence of the microcosmic point of view with the macrocosmic 'point of view'.[2] One must distinguish these 'objective'

---

[1] cf. the chapter on qualified space in *Le regne de la quantité et les signes des temps* of René Guénon.
[2] This coincidence of perspectives happens not only when one looks at one

17

directions, that is to say equal for all the terrestrial beings look-
ing at the sky at the same temporal instant, and the directions
one can call 'subjective' because these are determined by the
individual zenith and the nadir; we will point out in passing
that it is precisely this comparison between these two orders
of the directions of the celestial space that is the basis of the
horoscope. The indefinity of the directions of the space is in
itself undifferentiated, we mean to say that they have in them
virtually all the spatial relations possible without it being possible to define them. But the qualities of these directions of the
celestial space are interdependent; we mean that as soon as one
direction of the celestial space – or point of the limit-sphere
which corresponds to it – is defined, the whole of the other directions become differentiated and polarised with respect to that
one. It is in this sense that the Master says that the divisions of
the sky without stars or the sky of the zodiacal 'towers' are 'virtual determinations which are not differentiated except with respect to the sky of the 'stations' of the stars. However, the fixed
points of the sky of the 'stations' are above all the respective
poles of the diurnal revolution of the sky (or of the earth) and
of the annual cycle of the sun, and are consequently the points

point of the sky-limit, but even when one fixes on a planet. It is expressed
in current experience according to which each spectator who looks at the
sun rising or setting on the other side of an expanse of water sees the 'paths'
of the rays reflected in the water coming directly towards him; when the
spectator moves to another point, this luminous path follows him. – Let us
note in passing that the North American Indians consider this luminous path,
reflected on water by the rays of the setting sun, a path for the souls on their
return to the world of their ancestors; in fact, one can see in this a 'horizontal' projection of 'solar rays', which, according to the Hindu symbolism,
represents the tie by which each particular individual is attached directly to
his principal. We know that the sacred texts of Hinduism describe this ray
as going from the 'crown' of the head to the sun. The same symbolism –
implying at the same time the idea of a direct tie and that of the 'Divine Way'
– can be found in this passage from the Sura of Hûd: 'There does not exist a
living being whom He (Allah) does not hold by his forlock; in truth my
Lord is on a straight path'. – Like the 'Divine Way', the direction which goes
from any one of the terrestrial beings to a determined point of the celestial
vault is at the same time unique for each and the same for all.

that the divergence of these poles determine on the ecliptic, that is to say the two equinoxes, points of intersection of the solar orbit with the equator, on the one hand, and the two solstices, extreme points of the two phases, ascendant and descendant of the solar cycle, on the other hand. As soon as these four points of the ecliptic are fixed, the other eight zodiacal divisions respond to these by virtue of the ternary and senary partitions which are naturally inherent to the circle, as is expressed in the relationship between the rays and the proportions of the hexagon inscribed in the circle. Then it is as though a spontaneous crystallisation of spatial relations is produced, each point of the quaternary evokes two other points of a trigon, which in their turn repeat the relation in 'square', so that the division of the circle by four is thus integrated and compensated by a 'congenital' synthesis to the 'universal' nature of the cycle, according to the formula $3 \times 4 = 4 \times 3 = 12$.

If the two great circles, that of the celestial equator and that of the solar cycle, coincided, there would be no manifestation of the seasons. The divergence of the two great celestial cycles evidently expresses therefore the rupture of the equilibrium

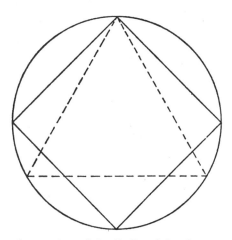

Generation of the Zodiacal duodenary
by the square and the trigon.

which engenders a certain order of manifestation, that is to say that of contrasts and of complementaries; and the four cardinal points determined by this divergence are obviously the signs or the marks of this contrast. Ibn 'Arabi identifies the zodiacal quaternary with that of the qualities or fundamental tendencies of the total or universal Nature (*at-tabi'ah*), which is the root of all the differentiations. Let us add, to prevent all possible misunderstanding, that the Total Nature such as the Master envisages is not the Universal Substance as such, the first passive principle that the Hindu doctrine calls *Prakriti* and that Muhyiddin Ibn 'Arabi designates either by the term of *al-habâ* ('Substance'), or by *al-'unsur al-a'zam* ('Supreme Element'), but that it is a direct determination envisaged more particularly under its aspect of 'maternity' with regard to the creatures. The Universal Nature, non-manifested in itself, manifests itself by four qualities or fundamental tendencies which appear in the sensible order as heat and cold, dryness and humidity. The heat and cold are active qualities opposed one to the other; they manifest also as expansive forces and contractive forces; they determine the pair of passive qualities, the dryness and humidity. Taken to the four cardinal points of the zodiac, the cold corresponds to the two solstices, which reflect in some ways the polar contraction, whereas the heat corresponds to the two equinoxes which are situated on the equator, pitch of the expansion of the celestial movements. Because of this fact, the cardinal signs succeed each other by contrasts; but the passive qualities of dryness and humidity tie together two pairs of these. The four tendencies or qualities of Nature are joined two by two in the nature of the four elements or foundation of the sensible world, produced starting with the terrestrial substance: earth is cold and dry, water is cold and humid, air is humid and hot, fire is hot and dry. If one attributes these elementary qualities to the signs of the zodiac saying that Aries is

[3] The traditional medicine of the Moslem world reduces all the illnesses to so many manifestations of disequilibrium of these four tendencies.

of igneous nature, Cancer aqueous, Libra aerial and Capricorn earthly, one must take account of the fact that the zodiac contains only the celestial models of the four elements and that these models remain composed of four tendencies of the Total Nature, just as Muhyiddin Ibn 'Arabi points out.

The quaternary of the fundamental tendencies of the Total Nature should be multiplied, according to Muhyiddin Ibn 'Arabi, by the ternary whose cosmic congenitors are the three movements or principial orientations of the First Intellect or Universal Spirit (al-'aql), or even under another relationship, the three worlds, that is to say, the present world, the future world and the intermediary state of barzakh.[4] The three movements or orientations of the Spirit are : the descending movement, which obviously recedes from the Principle and which measures the depths (al-'umq) of the possible; the expansive movement, which measures its amplitude or width (al-'urd); the movement of return towards the origin, which is directive in the sense of the exaltation or the height (at-tûl). This ternary of the Spirit is superior to the quaternary of the Nature; if it appears here in the second place, this is because the differentiations of the zodiacal sky of the archetypes proceed from manifested contrasts to arrive at their reintegration in the perfect synthesis. As a result of this reintegration all multiplication, all points of the zodiac which happen to be in relation to the trigon have the same elementary nature but are distinguished by the qualities relevant to the ternary of the Spirit; and all the points which happen to be in relation to the square have the same spiritual quality but are differentiated by the elementary contrasts. From this one can already deduce the different characters of the 'aspects' or reciprocal positions of the planets on the ecliptic : the relation in right angles necessarily denotes contrast, in the same way that opposition signifies opposition; the trigon is the expression of a perfect synthesis, and the sextile, that is to say the

[4] On the different significances of this word, see our article 'Du barzakh', in Etudes Traditionelles Dec. 1937.

position at an angle of 60 degrees, expresses an affinity. Applied to the nature of the cycle, the three principial movements of the Spirit can no more be compared to the three dimensions of depth, amplitude and height, but they appear in accordance with a reflection conforming to this nature : the only tendency which is directly manifested in the cyclic order is that of the expansion in amplitude, because the cycle is before anything else an image of the development of all the possibilities implied in the amplitude of a degree of manifestation. In conformity with this, the cardinal signs, critical regions of the solar cycle, are called 'mobiles' (*munqalib*), that is to say dynamics or expansives. As for the descendent movements of the Spirit, it is translated in the cyclic order by fixation (*sukûn*), and it is because of this 'movement' that the world subsists as such. At last, the spiritual movements of return towards the origin is reflected in the plane of the zodiacal cycle by the synthesis of the two other orientations, and the signs co-ordinated with them are called 'doubles' or 'synthetics' (*dhû ishtirâh*). We ought to point out in passing that these ternary determinations of the zodiac come from an altogether different perspective on the symbolism of the two phases, ascendent and descendent, of the solar cycle, a symbolism which can evidently be attached to the two movements or opposed orientations of the Spirit; but here it has to do with a dualism which is related to a cyclic movement, whereas the ternary that we have just described is attached to an 'existential' determination of the cycle. The expression of 'movement' to indicate the orientations of the Universal Spirit, should be taken in a purely symbolic sense.

As to the correspondences with the three worlds or degrees of human existence, such as appear in the symbolism of the angelic functions to which are related the twelve zodiacal signs, a symbolism which we have extracted from the book 'The Tie which Retains the Departing' (*'uglat al-mustawfiz*) of Muhyiddin Ibn 'Arabi, as to these correspondences, as we were saying, they should be understood starting with the reflections of the

22

intellectual terrain in the nature of the cycle, and according to the perspective of the production of these three worlds. This explains why it is not the 'synthetic' signs attributed to the ascendent orientation of Spirit, which regulate the relatively superior world, that is to say the intemporal degrees of the human state, but the 'fixed' signs; on the other hand it is evident that it is the 'mobile' signs which are related to the development of the states of this world. As to the synthetic signs or 'doubles', they correspond to the intermediary worlds (the *barzakh* of the Islamic theology, the Christian purgatory and the Tibetan *bardo*), or again, according to a slightly different perspective, to the synthesis of the spiritual immutability and psychic expansivity in the corporal composition – in the same manner as the production of the alchemical salt by the union of sulphur and of mercury.

I. MOBILE SIGNS

Aries is of hot and dry nature (igneous). Its angel holds the keys of the creation of qualities and of accidents.

Cancer is of cold and humid nature (aqueous). Its angel holds the keys of the creation of this world.

Libra is of hot and humid nature (aerial). Its angel holds the keys of the creation of states (ephemeral) and of changes.

Capricorn is of cold and dry nature (earthly). Its angel holds the keys of day and night.

II. FIXED SIGNS

Taurus is of cold and dry nature (earthly). Its angel holds the keys of the creation of paradise and of hell, and it is under the terror of the Majesty (*haybah*).

Leo is of hot and dry nature (igneous). Its angel is generous (*karîm*); he holds the keys of the creation of the future world.

Scorpio is of cold and humid nature (aqueous). Its angel holds the keys of the creation of fire (infernal).

Aquarius is of hot and humid nature (aerial). Its angel is generous, and is under the terror of the Majesty; he holds the keys of the spirits.

III. SYNTHETIC SIGNS

Gemini are of hot and humid nature (aerial). Their angel rules the bodies in communion with the rectors of the other double signs; he holds in particular the key to the creation of metals.

Virgo is of cold and dry nature (terrestrial). Its angel rules, in communion with the other double signs, the bodies, and in particular the human body.

Sagittarius is of hot and dry nature (igneous). Its angel is generous; it rules the luminous bodies and the tenebrous bodies, and it holds in particular the key to the creation of plants.

Pisces are of cold and humid nature (aqueous). Their angel rules, in communion with the other angels of bodies, luminous bodies and the tenebrous bodies and in particular it holds the keys to the creation of animals.

We have now exposed, in general terms, the differentiation of the twelve regions of the zodiac of the sky-limit, beginning with the fixed points of the solar cycle. We shall again point out that this way of conceiving the division of the zodiac justifies the manner currently employed in Arab and Occidental astrology of situating the twelve signs; this manner consists of counting twelve equal parts, beginning with the Spring Equinox, with abstraction made of the situation of the constellations carrying the same names as the signs; because, due to the precession of the equinoxes, each of which makes the tour of the whole sky in about 26,000 years, a discrepancy has resulted of nearly a whole 'sign' between the situation of the constellations and the parts of the zodiac having the same name; the constellation of Aries, for example, is today to be found in the 'sign' of Taurus. One could bring up the question of knowing whether the form of these groupings of the fixed stars, which were at the origin points of reference for the determination of the twelve parts of the solar cycle, is indifferent with respect to the meaning of these; yet surely there is analogy between the denomination of the zodiacal signs and these groupings of stars on the ecliptic: the constellation of Gemini is characterised effectively by a couple of twin stars; that of Taurus contains a triangle resembling the head of the animal, and the shapes of Scorpio and of Leo can be recognised in the constellations of the same names, even though other interpretations of these groupings are equally conceivable. On the other hand, it is quite likely that during the first fixation of the astrological symbols the resemblances were more striking, because certain 'fixed' stars must surely have moved since that very far distant time,[5] as Muhyiddin Ibn' Arabi points out by referring to certain stellar representations on the monuments of ancient Egypt. Originally, the symbolic images attributed to the twelve parts of the solar cycle would have presented a synthesis between, on the one hand, the spiritual significance of these determinations of celestial space, and on the other hand, the possible interpretations of the groups of stars of the twelve constellations, the former playing an essential role, and the latent combinations of groups of stars – including their colours and their intensities – a potential role; once the fixation is done it would be imprinted in the collective memory by virtue of its originality both spiritual and imaginative; and this is in fact a particularly adequate image of a certain order of inspirations.

On the other hand, the precession of equinoxes, which constitute the major astronomical cycle, must necessarily play a role in the astrological symbolism, and the change of the place of the zodiacal constellations ought to be a part of its significance, to which matter we shall return later.

[5] The last coincidence of the zodiacal signs with the constellations of the same signs took place in the first century of the Christian era but it is probable that the denomination of the twelve constellations dates from a preceding coincidence. We shall come back to this matter.

III

THE HEAVEN of the fixed stars, which is contained in the sphere of the 'towers' of the zodiac, is called the heaven of the 'stations' (*manâzil*), because the movements of the planets project themselves upon it. The seven planets, which represent the cosmic intermediaries between the immutable world of the archetypes and the earthly centre, actualise, by their combined rhythms and the reciprocal positions which ensue, the spatial relations virtually contained in the indefinite sphere of the sky-limit, the sphere being no other than the totality of the directions of the space and hence the image of the universe.[1]

The modern astrologers would like to have it that the planets act on earth through rays of force, and they mean this in the material or quasi-material sense, because inevitably this introduces into astrology something of the modern conceptions of causality; and thence the residue of the science takes on the aspect of a true superstition. The need for causality depends on the general preoccupations of an era; it is true that it is always logical in the essence, because that which gives causal linkage its convincing character resides equally in the unity of the thought and in the nature of the things; but at the same time, the need for causality substantially depends on the mental level which is mechanistic or imaginative, reasoning or intuitive. As the mental horizon cannot englobe at a given time, except a cer-

[1] Whence the etymological derivation of the term 'universe' from *orbis universum*.

tain order of realities, the causal argument of an era mentally different, it appears insufficient or even defective, because one can see the limits of its development only in the sense of an ulterior investigation; one forgets only too easily that all causal linkage within manifestation is essentially symbolic,[2] and that the most vast and the most adequate conception of causality is precisely the one which is conscious of this symbolism and which considers all things within the relationship of the 'Unity of Existence' (wahdat-al-wujud). On the other hand, one must tell oneself that the essential reality of an intellectual perspective does not hinder its mental expression from remaining subject to the relativity of the exterior modes of knowledge; thus, for instance, Muhyiddin Ibn 'Arabi affirms of the sun – the 'heart of the world' – that it communicates light to all the other stars, including the fixed stars, and that it itself is illuminated by the direct and incessant irradiation of a Divine Revelation.[3]

This conception is essentially true, in the sense that all sensible light has its source in the intelligible light of which the sun is the most evident symbol; it is also true in the sense that the lights of the stars are of the same substance, as all modern astronomers recognise; and finally it is true that the sun communicates its light to all the planets. As to the fixed stars, one is today convinced that they represent sources of light independent of the sun, and on this point the conception of Muhyiddin Ibn 'Arabi may appear mistaken; however the function of a Master in Metaphysics does not necessarily imply a distinctive knowledge of all the domains of nature, and Ibn 'Arabi could not have envisaged the symbolism of astronomical knowledge in any other way than it presented itself to him. Of course this does not mean that his theory is no longer viable once one accepts that the fixed stars are autonomous lights in the sen-

---

[2] That is to say, the 'secondary causes' are nothing but the reflections of the 'first cause' and have no reality of their own.

[3] It is a significant fact that the eye cannot look at the sun – which illuminates the whole world – without being dazzled.

sible order, because the distinction between the totality of the stars ruled by the sun and the multitude of the fixed stars appears only like a differentiation of the same symbolism, in the sense that the sun represents the centre of radiation of the Divine Light for a determined world, whereas the fixed stars symbolise the interferences of the light of a superior world; but even in this case one could say that the light which radiates from the sun is the same as that which illuminates all the celestial bodies.

This diversion of different perspectives, according to which one can envisage the cosmic causality, was necessary so as to situate the role of the planets in astrology and to make clear what one should understand by the influence of their radiation. Whatever may be the material or subtle effects of their rays, the contemplative penetration of the 'physiognomy' of the cosmos considers them more directly as modes of the Intellect in its macrocosmic manifestation, modes which realise or measure the possibilities contained in the indefinite sphere. The celestial space in which the planets describe their revolutions represents in some ways the extreme limits of the sensible world, and these limits are inversely analogous to the centre which is man himself, just as we have already pointed out by considering the 'objective' character of the spatial directions radiating from each human being towards the same point of the sky-limit;[4] because of this inverse analogy, the modes of the Cosmic Intellect represented by the stars are 'existential' instead of being 'intelligent', this last word to be taken in the sense of the active intelligence manifesting in man; here we refer to the polarity of 'existence' and 'intelligence' in the Being.[5]

[4] There will perhaps be objections that the directions which we call 'objective' only depend upon the 'collective subjectivity'; but in the order of direct and spontaneous sensory perception, on which this symbolism in question is based, this 'collective subjectivity' is the equivalent of 'objectivity'. See Frithjof Schuon on this matter in his article entitled *Fatalité et Progrès*: the passage we have reproduced as a footnote earlier in this study.

[5] cf. Frithjof Schuon's article: 'Transcendence et Universalité de l'Esoterism' in the *Etudes Traditionelles* of October to November 1945.

This intellectual nature of the planets is expressed – always because of that same inverse analogy with reference to the active intelligence – in the regularity and rhythmic continuity of their movements. Their luminous nature depends on the same symbolism; on the other hand, the propagation of light is so to speak 'geometric' and corresponds to the actualisation of the directions and spatial relations. It is necessary to understand well that the symbolism does not envisage the situation of the planets in the quantitatively measurable space; their 'aspects' are determined by their projection on the zodiac, that is to say, by reason of the directions of the space, the centre of which is the terrestrial human being. As to the directions of the space, their definition is obviously not quantitative but always relative to the indivisible unity of the indefinite sphere of the extreme sky.

Of all the 'mobile' stars, only the movements of the Sun and the Moon can be represented by regular circles on the sky of the fixed stars, because the apparent orbits of the other planets are ruled at the same time by the solar centre and the terrestrial centre, so that they revolve in combined movements. There is, then, a simple interaction between the solar rhythms and those of the moon; this latter traverses the zodiac in 28 days and it is assigned 28 stations or houses which are spread in an unequal but rhythmic fashion over the twelve paths of the zodiac, and which one counts beginning with the Spring Equinox. The true beginning of the lunar cycle, which expresses itself through the succession of lunations, does not always coincide with the point of the equinox; because the two points of interception of the lunar orbit with the solar cycle, which are called the 'head' and the 'tail' of the dragon, describes in 18 years the circle of all the 'sky of stations'. The fixing of the mansions of the moon, therefore, consists of a sort of symbolic summary of the real rhythms.[*]

[*] The Hindu astrology considers only 27 lunar mansions, the course of the Moon around the sky not taking place in complete numbers of days, so that

In the relationship between the lunar mansions and the zodiac is manifested an evident numerical symbolism; we have shown how the zodiacal duodenary presents itself as a product of the multiplication of the quaternary by the ternary; however, multiplication symbolises the mode of distinction peculiar to the world of archetypes, because these are not differentiated by mutual exclusion but in the manner of mirrors that reflect each other and do not differ except by their reciprocal position. The same numbers 3 and 4 compose also the number of the seven planets of astrology; and as the planets are the intermediaries between the sky of the archetypes and the earth, their distinction is that of a hierarchy and contains the principles of the ternary and of the quaternary according to the gradual order. As to the number 28 of the houses of the moon, this is obtained by the Pythagorician sum of numbers from 1 to 7, with signifies that the lunar rhythm develops or exposes, in a successive mode, all the possibilities contained in the archetypes and transmitted, by the hierarchy of the intermediaries, to the sphere which immediately surrounds the terrestrial centre.

The relation between the Sun and the Moon is analogous to that which holds between the Pure Intellect and its reflection in the human form. This also finds its most evident expression in the fact that the Moon reflects the radiation of the Sun in the manner of a mirror, and that the cycle of the lunations is like a 'discursive' development of this radiation. But the same symbolism appears also in the relationship of the movements of the two astral bodies; we have already exposed above that it is the Sun which by its movements actualises or measures the virtual determinations of the zodiacal sky of archetypes, be-

the symbolic summary of its cycle can either be taken up to 28 days or reduced to 27 days. On the other hand, the Hindu astrologers do not situate the beginning of the lunar cycle at the point of the actual vernal, but at the point of the sky of fixed stars, which coincided at the time of the last coincidence between the zodiacal signs and the synonymous constellations, with the Spring Equinox. We shall come back on this difference of points of view.

cause without the fixed points of the solar cycle the directions of the sky without stars would be undefinable. The Sun measures, therefore, the celestial space in an active fashion, in the same way that the essential act of the Intellect represents the *fiat lux* which extracts the world of shadows from the potential indifferentiation; on the other hand, the Moon measures the sky passively by traversing the solar zodiac; she is subject at the same time to the determinations of the directions of celestial space and to the directions of the solar rays, a double dependence which translates itself in her luminous phases and in the regular rhythm of the 18 years, according to which her cycle is displaced in relation to that of the zodiac. We shall see later on that the directions of space, whose influence the Moon suffers one by one, correspond to so many qualities of the Being.

The fact that the Moon is the receptacle for all the influences that she collects to transmit to the Earth is also shown by the degree which corresponds to the Moon in the hierarchy of the prophetic function; the Islamic esotericism, we know, 'situates' these functions symbolically in the different planetary skies. According to this order of correspondences, which however cannot be understood except within their spiritual perspective and in some way within the 'cyclic' of Islam,[7] Abraham (*Seyid-na Ibrahim*) resides in the sky of Saturn, Moses (*Seyid-na Musa*) in that of Jupiter, Aaron (*Seyid-na Harun*) in that of Mars, Enoch (*Seyid-na Idris*) in that of the Sun, Joseph (*Seyid-na Yusuf*) in that of Venus, Jesus (*Seyid-na 'Isa*) in that of Mercury and Adam (*Seyid-na Adam*) in that of the Moon. There is in this hierarchy the same relationship between Enoch and Adam as exists between the 'transcendent man' (*shoen jen*) and the 'true man' (*chen jen*) in the Taoist doctrine: Enoch resides in the

[7] From this one could conclude that the spiritual interpretation of astrology could not be transferred from one tradition to another. Not only does this interpretation belong to an intellectual perspective proper to a tradition, but even the validity of its divinatory applications depends in a certain measure on the homogeneity of the subtle atmosphere ruled by the spiritual influence of the envisaged tradition.

Sun because he represents the 'divine man' par excellence, or the first 'spiritual great' of the sons of Adam, and consequently the 'historic prototype' of all men that have realised God. As for Adam, he is the 'primordial man' or, according to the expression of Ibn 'Arabi, the 'unique man' (al-insan al-mufrad, as opposed to al-insan al-kâmil, the 'universal man'), that is to say he is the representative par excellence of the cosmic quality which belongs to man alone, and which expresses itself in the role of the mediator between 'earth' and 'Heaven'. Ibn 'Arabi compares the Moon to the heart of the 'unique man', which receives the revelation (tajallî) of the Divine Essence (dhat); this heart changes form continually according to the different 'essential truths' (haqâiq) which leave successively therein their imprint. The fact that the Master speaks of the heart indicates that here it has to do not with the mental, a faculty purely discursive, but on the contrary, with the central organ of the soul; the continual change of form which this heart undergoes should not be confused with the translation in discursive mode, operated by the mental, of a spiritual knowledge, even though the central and mediatorial role of reason evidently relates to the same cosmic quality which characterises the human being. From another point of view, the description of this continual renewing of the heart, or rather of its form, shows that it is not identical under all its aspects to the transcendent pole of the being – the Intellect – and that it is as if it were circumscribed by the limits of the individual substance, which, this latter, could not receive simultaneously all the aspects implied in the inexhaustible actuality of the 'Essential Revelation' (tajallî dhatî); because of this the subtle form of the heart changes all the time, successively answering all the directions or spiritual polarisations, and this change is at once comparable both to a pulsation and to phases of the Moon. The incessant evolution in the forms is like the exterior and inversed image of the immutable interior orientation of the heart of the 'unique man', because, being always open only to the transcendent Unity, and being always conscious of what It alone reveals in all the qualities of the Intellectual Light, the heart could never remain closed or immobilised in one single form; and it is precisely in this that the double aspect of the role of the mediator proper to the human heart consists.

Now, it is to this faculty of mediation that relates the transformation of the primordial sound, which is the vehicle of the spiritual revelation, in articulated language. It is for this reason that Islamic esotericism establishes a correspondence between the 28 mansions of the Moon and the 28 letters or sounds of the sacred language. 'It is not like people think,' – says Muhyid-din Ibn 'Arabi, – 'that the mansions of the Moon represent the models of the letters; it is the 28 sounds which determine the lunar mansions." These sounds represent in fact the microcosmic and human expression of the essential determinations of the Divine Breath, which is itself the prime motivation of cosmic cycles. The Master counts the 28 sounds of the Arabic alphabet from the first lunar mansion, which follows the Spring Equinox, in the successive order of their phonetic exteriorisation, beginning with the hiatus (al-hamzah), and going on through the gutteral consonants to the labials passing through the palatals and the dentals. If one takes into account the fact that the initial hiatus is not properly speaking a sound, but only a transitory instant between silence and locution, the series of sounds attributed to the lunar mansions begins with the *hâ* and ends with the *waw*, these two letters composing the Divine Name *huwa*, 'He', symbol of the Essence one and identical to Itself.

IV

THE MOST profound significance of astronomical cycles consists in the fact that they offer an image logically analogous to all successive developments of possibilities ruled by the pole of one and the same principle, so that they symbolise no matter which order of manifestation, be it that that order is conditioned by time or be it that the succession it implies is of a purely logical nature. Consequently it is possible to conceive of a whole hierarchy of cosmic 'cycles' analogous among themselves, but situated at different levels of existence and each reflected simultaneously and in different relationships, in an astronomical cycle such as the one traversed by the Sun or the Moon on the sky of the fixed stars. In his book 'The Revelations of Mecca' (*al-futuhat al-makkiyah*), Muhyiddin Ibn 'Arabi cites a series of cosmological correspondences which allows the tracing of a symbolic diagram which will be found as an inset in this book. This diagram is built upon the juxtaposition of the zodiac and the cycle of the lunar mansions, beginning with the Spring Equinox, and the different orders of analogies are indicated by concentric circles.

The first reason of all cycles of manifestation is the deployment of the principial possibilities of manifestation, symbolised by the series of Divine Names. On the other hand, the science of the Names or the Divine Qualities – the former being no other than the logical determinations of the latter – constitute the supreme conclusion of all sacred science, because universal

36

qualities are in some ways the distinctive contents of the Divine Essence, whereas the Divine Essence in Itself can never be the object of a science, that is to say the object of a knowledge which could yet again imply what so ever distinction. The qualities or the Divine Names are necessarily innumerable; but due to the simplicity of this Being, which is one of the aspects of Its Unity, they can be symbolically summarised in a determined group, which would all the same be more or less numerically large, according to the principles of logical differentiation that one would like to apply. As there is no distinction without implicit hierarchy, the series of Names would always have the character of a logical chain, and it is by this that it becomes the model of all cyclic order.

In the present case, the Master makes the 28 mansions of the Moon correspond to as many Divine Names. On the other hand, these, which all have an active or creative character, have as complements or as direct objects the same number of cosmic degrees, so that their connection forms a second analogous cycle. The series of these cosmic degrees produced by the series of the Divine Names go from the first manifestation of the Intellect down to the creation of man. In its hierarchy it also comprises the cosmic degrees which correspond to the different heavens, that is to say to the heavens of the zodiac, to the heavens of the fixed stars, and to the seven planetary skies. But these degrees which are here related to certain regions of the zodiac, measured by lunar mansions, should in reality be conceived as a 'vertical' succession in relation to the zodiacal cycle, and one must understand well that there is, in this attribution of a series of cosmic degrees to the lunar 'stations' and consequently to the zodiacal regions, something like a projection of a 'vertical' hierarchy on a 'horizontal' plane.

The Divine Names represent the determining essences of the corresponding cosmic domains. As to the production of these domains, starting with their principial determinations, it is the effects of the Divine Breath (an-nafas al-ilâhî), which

37

deploys all the possibilities of manifestation implied in the principial determinations of the Names. According to a symbolism which is at the same time verbal and figurative, before the creation of the world the Divine Names were in a state of divine constriction (*al-karb al-ilâhî*), and then they 'demand' their created complements, until the Divine Spirit 'relieved' (*tanaffasa*) them, by deploying all the amplitude of their consequences. In other words, as soon as the Being conceives, in Its first auto-determination (*ta 'ayyun*), the principal distinctions which are His Names or His Qualities, these require their logical complements, the totality of which will constitute the world. It is the Divine Breath which 'extends' this logical connection in an existential manner, and it identifies itself in this respect to the First Substance and to Universal Nature. It is thus that we can summarise in a few words the theory of the Divine Breath, a theory which takes into account the symbolic correspondence which ties together between themselves the cycle of the Divine Names, that of the cosmic degrees and that of the 28 sounds of the Arabic alphabet, the cosmic degrees being the determinations of the Universal and Macrocosmic Breath and the 28 sounds those of the human and microcosmic breath; the sounds of the language are carried by the physical breath, just as the cosmic degrees are 'carried' by the Divine 'expansion'. We have explained above the reason for the analogy which relates these 28 sounds to the lunar sphere.

The Master points out that the hierarchy of the cosmic degrees that he enumerates according to the order of the lunar mansions, should not be understood as a series of successive productions, but as a definite scale of degrees of existence; because the order of production does not correspond to the definitive hierarchy; it is inverse according to whether it is the degrees of universal and informal existence, or the degrees inferior to the sky of the fixed stars, that is to say the degrees of the individual world, and this is easily understandable, seeing that the production of the superior states cannot be conceived except in a purely logical fashion, in the sense of an essential differentiation beginning with the Unity of the Being; the production of the formal and individual worlds, on the other hand, would necessarily be envisaged with respect to their substantial reality, or even 'material', therefore like an opening up of forms and states of existence, beginning with the potentiality of an undifferentiated *materia*, which, because of its shadowy passivity, is situated at the lower degree of an ascending scale of states of existence. Therefore the result of this is that the ontological level of the Prime Matter, or of the plastic substance of the body of manifestations, can be conceived and represented in different ways, according to whether one considers it as the first term of a series of successive productions, or as the beginning of the series because all the successive entities draw their plastic substance from it, or again whether one assigns to it the last level of a static hierarchy or whether it will play a role in the inferior root or whether it is as the anchor thrown into an abysmal depth.

This double hierarchical situation of the Prime Matter, or of the passive substance, is expressed in the level that it occupies in the cosmological schemata which we will study, the principal that Muhyiddin Ibn 'Arabi calls *al-jawhar al-habâi* – which corresponds to the Prime Matter – or again *al-hayûlâ*, the Arabic term for '*hylé*'. The Master writes that this cosmic entity here holds the fourth level because it is the necessary premise of the following level, assigned to 'Universal Body', secondary substance, which fills the intelligible 'space' as ether, or the *akâsha* of the Hindu doctrine, fills the sensible space. It is in this respect, that is to say as the immediate origin of 'Universal Body', that cosmology generally conceives of the reality of the Prime Matter. Nevertheless, according to its most profound meaning which Muhyiddin Ibn 'Arabi exposes, the Prime Matter, conceived as the Universal Substance which is the support of all the principial determinations, should be represented outside this hierarchical succession, because it is either superior or inferior to all the other degrees; its place in the interior of the hierarchy is all the same justified by the fact that it represents the last term of the first quaternary which summarises in itself alone all Universal Existence: the Universal Soul (*an-nafs al-kulliyah*), which occupies the second degree, is in some way a result of the action of the First Intellect (*al-'aql*) on the First Substance (*al-Habâ*); and Universal Nature (*at-tabî 'ah*), which is situated at the third level, appears like a modification of this substance. On the other hand, the Prime Matter (*al-jawhar al-habâi*) is attributed to the Divine Name 'the Last' (*al-akhir*), which expresses the divine 'faculty' of being 'Last' without temporal ulteriority, or being 'other' without essential altereity, this meaning obviously corresponding to the function of the passive substance which is the indefinable root of all manifestation.

This explanation of the hierarchical level of the Prime Matter was necessary in order to indicate how one should envisage the cosmic degrees of succession. As to the other terms of this same hierarchy, their explanation would take us beyond the framework of this study; we will limit ourselves therefore to the indication of some general distinctions. One will notice that the cycle of the Names of the cosmic degrees and the lunar mansions can be divided into quarters, each of which comprises seven mansions corresponding to a definite total of degrees of existence: the first quarter symbolises the world of principals or the totality of Divine Degrees: this quarter is symbolically terminated at the Summer Solstice, and at the degree of the Divine 'Throne', which is the complement of the Divine Name *al-muhit*, 'He who englobes all', is the model of the letter *qaf*, sign of the pole and name of the polar mountains that the Hindus call *Merû*; and, let us add, in there it is as if it were a verbal image of the fact that the Divine 'Throne' is at the same time the sphere which englobes all and the pole around which revolves the circumambulation of the angels. The next two quarters symbolise all the formal worlds, but in only one respect, that of the 'elementary' and direct existence of each of their degrees; because it is the last quarter of the cycle which represents the hierarchy of the composite beings, that is to say beings whose forms draw from a synthesis of many degrees of existence. The two middle quarters constitute therefore a single 'world'; but they can be divided with respect to the centre of this world, this centre being the sphere of the Sun, which is the 'heart of the world', and which is here placed in analogical relation to the Autumn Equinox.

The 'intermediary' world comprises the seven planetary skies, and their attribution to an equal number of Divine Names indicates with precision the cosmic principles of which the planetary rhythms are an expression.

The sky of Saturn is attributed to the Divine Name *ar-Rabb*, 'the Lord', the meaning of which implies a reciprocal relationship, because a being has no quality of lordship except in relation to a servant, and the servant is not thus a servant except in relation to a lord. For the created being, this relationship has a necessary and unalterable character whereas the other divine qualities can in some ways vary in colour according to the individual. The sky of Jupiter is the complement of the Divine Name *al-alîm*, 'the Knower' or 'the Learned'. Mars corresponds to the Divine Name *al-qâhir*, 'the Conqueror' or 'the Tamer'; Jupiter reigns over the intellectual faculty and Mars the volitive faculty. The Sun is analogous to the Divine Name *an-nûr*, 'the Light', whereas the Moon corresponds to the Divine Name *al-mubîn*, 'the Apparent' or 'the Evident'. The Sun symbolises the principal of Intellect itself, whereas the Moon represents manifestation; there is between these two names the same relationship as that between 'Truth' and 'Proof', or between 'Revelation' and 'Commentary'. Venus is attributed to the Divine Name *al-musawwir*, He who forms, a word which equally signifies the painter and the sculptor, and the feminine form of which signifies the imaginative faculty. As for Mercury, it is the analogy of the Divine Name *al-muhsi*, 'He who counts', the the significance of which is related to numbers and to distinctive knowledge.[1]

The two middle quarters of the cycle, symbolised by the zodiacal hemicycle situated between the Summer and Winter Solstices, englobes all the hierarchy of the celestial spheres, starting in an ascending order with the Divine 'Throne'; and this hemicycle effectively corresponds to the descendent phase of the solar trajectory. The last mansion before the Winter Solstice is attributed to the element earth; the point itself of the Solstice symbolises therefore the centre of gravity, lowest point which would be the level of the passive matter of the human world – not of the Prime Matter of all the universe – because this centre of gravity is not the lowest point except with respect to the world of men. From this point on, the meaning of the hierarchical order changes and becomes ascending, going from the elementary towards synthesis. First comes the three kingdoms of minerals (or metals, because the pure mineral is always reduced to metal), of plants, and of animals, and after that the degrees of angels, genii, and men. It would seem strange that the angels should precede the genii (*jinn*); since the genii belong only to the psychic world, whereas the angels belong to the informal world and thereby should surpass them in knowledge and in power; but the order of succession goes from that which is more simple towards that which is more composite, from that which is less individualised towards individuation. Because of this, man represents the last synthesis in this world, because the cyclic degree which follows and which terminates all the hierarchy is no more, to be precise, a degree of existence; it symbolises the reintegration of all the preceding degrees in the First Intellect. Therefore the Master says of this last mansion of the cycle that it corresponds to the 'determination of all the degrees', that is to say to their

---

[1] This refers to a perspective other than the one which envisages the prophetic functions in their correspondences with the seven planets.

intellectual hierarchisation, 'but not to their manifestation'. This hierarchisation identifies itself on the other hand to the 'Universal Man (*al-insan al-kâmil*), whose existence is purely virtual with respect to the domain of distinctive manifestation, being as it were the ideal model of the return of man to the Principle.

From another point of view, one should not lose sight of the fact that this cosmological hierarchy, projected into a cycle, is at the same time determined by the encatonation of macrocosmic degrees and by the human perspective : this is perfectly licit, given that the human being occupies a central position in the cosmic atmosphere which surrounds him, and that he has a right to consider this position, since he is obliged to make of it a starting point for his spiritual realisation, as he is situated on the axis itself which unites the poles of the universe, passing from the lowest centre of 'material' gravity up to the supreme centre of 'First Intellect'.

The system of correspondences that Muhyiddin Ibn 'Arabi gives us permits us to relate each mansion of the Moon to a Divine Quality; on the other hand, these mansions are superimposed on the twelve zodiacal regions, according to an unequal but rhythmic superimposition, and in a manner where each zodiacal sign comprises seven-thirds of lunar mansions. We still have to consider the following modes according to which the cosmic and intellectual qualities of these mansions are combined, so as to give the qualities inherent to the zodiacal regions.

V

THE DIRECTIONS of this space are particularly adequate symbols for the nature of the Divine Qualities. Like these Qualities, which are the first determinations of the Being, the directions of this space are in an inexhaustible multitude; one cannot, however, conceive of them as a multitude, because each direction is in itself perfectly determined, its sole reason of existence being precisely the singularity of its determination.

Likewise for the Divine Qualities, the totality of directions of the space cannot be defined, and the unlimited sphere, the logical form of their extreme radiation, is no other than a symbol which is imposed on the mind without one knowing how to prove it. Whether it is the Divine Qualities or the directions of the space, as soon as one among them is 'named', the others can then be defined by their relationship to this, which is an aspect of the Unicity of Existence.

When one gives an image to the Divine Qualities, the centre of their radiation must be identified with the unconditional Principle. As for the directions of the celestial space, their centre is the human being – or each human being existing on earth – without this implying a plurality of centres, as we have already explained. There is therefore an inverse analogy between the logical image of the Divine Qualities and the directions of the celestial space.

In principal it is the Spirit present in man which is both the Divine centre from which radiates the qualities of the space,

44

and the limit-sphere which synthesises these; but in fact, the human spirit is subjected to the convergent rays of the celestial vault; because man, not actually being identified with his increated centre, is submitted to the totality of the Spirit as a reality or as a destiny exterior to himself. It is in this way that the sky react⁵ upon the relative eccentricity of the individual nature, eccentricity which is symbolically expressed by the situation of the 'subjective' directions of space at the moment of birth.

A sheaf of directions or of qualities can always be replaced by a single one which is in some way the resultant; meanwhile this resultant is not presented as a sum or a mixture of directions or qualities that is summarises, because though this is a synthesis of all the others, it is also a unique thing in itself, since the singularity of the determination constitutes the essential character of each direction; it implies therefore a new quality which the sum of the preceding qualities cannot express.

This law, which is full of cosmological consequences, should also be applied to the combination of several natures of the lunar mansions in one zodiacal sign. Each lunar mansion represents a sheaf of directions of celestial space, the synthesis of which symbolically corresponds to one Divine Quality. These sheaves fall unequally on the twelve regions of the zodiac, in such a way that each zodiacal sign comprises either two complete mansions and a third of a mansion, or only one complete mansion with on either side of it two thirds of a mansion. The signs of the first category are called 'pure' signs, and those of the second, 'mixed'. Now, according to Muhyiddin Ibn 'Arabi, the qualities of the fractured mansions are combined on the one hand with the complementary fractions of the other mansions contained in the same sign, constituting together with these, new resultants, and they concur, thanks to their original qualities as well as to their new resultants, with the constitution of the synthesis which expresses the qualitative nature of the zodiacal sign in question.

45

This synthesis, says Muhyiddin Ibn 'Arabi, is the cosmic model of all logical deduction, this always having the form of two premises founded on two couples of terms: a = b and b = c, of which the mean term b constitutes the link through which operates, the synthesis: a = c.

The qualities of the lunar mansions, he explains, confer upon each zodiacal sign seven aspects, to which is added three aspects inherent in this sign – and deployed elsewhere in its trigon – which makes ten aspects to be multiplied by their triple relationship with the three principal degrees of existence.[1]

The world, says the Master, consists of the Unity of the United (ahadiyad-al-majmû), whereas the Divine Independence resides in the Unity of the Unique (ahadiyad-al-wâhid). But Unicity is reflected in the interior of the unified multiple, in the singularity of each resultant, exactly as we have seen in the case of the synthesis of the directions of the space; thus a child represents the synthesis of the natures of his father and mother, but he is at the same time a unique and new being, and it is his unicity which is his real reason for existence. In general each singular part of the cosmos has in it at the same time a relative aspect according to which it is shown as a combination of several pre-existent elements, and a unique aspect which is in a way its face turned towards its Eternal Principle, and which corresponds, in its most real sense, to that which this thing or this being is in the Divine Science.[2]

Each element of a cosmic whole is other by what it represents in itself, and other because it is related to a synthesis. Further, each resultant of a synthesis is not only determined by its component parts, but in its turn determines the latter, by reason of what it contains of the unique. Because of this, each cosmic

[1] From these multiplications result 30 aspects for each sign, which adds up to 360 for all the zodiac, the number of the current division of the circle in degrees.

[2] On the difference between the essential aspect and the substantial aspect of a being, see also the article by René Guénon: 'L'Etre et le milieu' in Le Voile D'Isis, Dec. 1935.

domain is comparable to a tissue of relationships where each intersecting line is at the same time a centre and a part of the whole.[3]

It follows for astrology as an art, that these procedures have on the one hand the character of an exact deduction or of a calculation, and that they suppose on the other hand an intuition 'from above' from which ensues the unique quality of each newly nascent form of combinations. Whereas the deduction or the combination is superstantial or 'horizontal', the recognition of the uniqueness of each resultant is essential or 'vertical'. In each work of a traditional art like astrology there intervenes therefore, an inspiration more or less direct and which generally depends on participation in a spiritual influence. In fact there is no real 'exact' science without such a 'vertical' intervention, and this because of the double aspect of each existent form, as we have just explained. On the other hand, the deductive combinations of a cosmological science such as astrology produce a mass of symbolic potentialities which are susceptible of attracting 'inspirations' of very different natures; this is especially the case for all that relates to the divinatory art, which can always, to the degree in which it is interested, attract insidious interferences. In other words, man cannot remove the veil of his ignorance except by or through something which transcends his individual will; for the individual curiosity, all 'oracle' remains equivocal and may even reinforce the error which constitutes the fatal trap of such destiny.

Dealing with the super-position of the parts of the zodiac upon the lunar mansions, Muhyiddin Ibn 'Arabi points out that one zodiacal 'tower' must necessarily unite in itself both a complete number and a fraction of a number of mansions, 'without which the development and the diminution cannot appear in the world of becoming'. This remark contains an allusion to a law which is affirmed in the mutual relations between all the

[3] The geometric lines of ornamentation of Arab art can all be considered as symbols of this 'unicity' of the cosmos.

cosmic cycles, and especially in the relations between the cycles of the Sun and of the Moon; because, not only the lunar mansions are not contained entirely in the parts of the zodiac, but also the yearly course of the sun does not coincide with an entire number of lunar cycles; as it is said in the Koran (*surat Ya Sîn*): 'It is not allowed for the Sun to reach the Moon, nor is it to the night to overtake the day, but each moves in a special sphere' – if the Sun reached the Moon, that is to say, if a complete rhythm of lunar revolutions could be contained in one solar cycle, so that the evolutions of their reciprocal relationships return to the starting point, their common cycle would be achieved; their manifestation would be re-absorbed in non-manifestation: 'The night would overtake the day'.

There must also be, in a certain measure, a repetition; in the 18-year intervals, the reciprocal positions of the Sun and the Moon in fact travel the same cycles; but these are woven in the whole of the planetary world, and are situated according to the new proportions with respect to the other stars.

What is expressed in this super-position of the rhythms is, on the one hand, that all cycle of manifestation contains a relative repetition, because it is made up of images of the same 'polar' archetype, images which are necessarily analogous among themselves; but on the other hand, it does not contain any effective repetition, since the creative essence of the archetype can never be exhausted by these images or symbols. – Analogy is the trace of the Unity, and the inexhaustible character is the reflection of the infinity of the Principle.

The same law of non-repetition, which requires that not any one cosmic cycle closes upon itself, is also expressed in some way at the extreme limits of the sensible world, in the precession of equinoxes which makes it so that the intersection points of the solar cycle with the celestial equator effectuates, in relation to the 'sky of the fixed stars', one complete revolution in one period of about 26,000 years; from where results the actual dislocation between the sign or the divisions of the zodiac

48

and the twelve constellations which carry the same names. – We have already shown that the qualitative differentiation of the regions or celestial directions which are expressed in the divisions of the zodiac proceeds from the four constant terms of the solar cycle, the equinoxes and the solstices, and that it is not right to say – as some modern astrologers do – that the Spring Equinox moves from the *sign* of Aries to the *sign* of Aquarius, since the signs are counted invariably beginning from the vernal point. On the other hand, one could say that the *constellation* of Aries is moved towards the *sign* of Taurus or that the vernal point, that is to say the Spring Equinox, has moved from the constellation of Aries to that of Pisces; and one ought to suppose that the change of the relationship between these two supreme skies, that of the zodiacal 'towers' and that of the fixed stars, has modified in a certain way that which one could call 'the influence of the sky'. All the same, we have not any spatial measure for determining the contents of this great extreme cycle which is transposed in the precession of the equinoxes, because we know neither their beginning nor their end, and if we make abstractions of the constant terms of the solar cycle, the qualities of the celestial regions become completely undefinable.[4]

[4] We must answer the objection that could be raised from the fact that the Hindu astrology, which seems to go back to the same origins as the Hermetic astrology, does not refer, for the determination of the planetary positions, to the actual division of the zodiac beginning with the Spring Equinox (the vernal point), but to the twelve constellations of the sphere of the fixed stars. It would be erroneous to conclude from this that, according to one traditional point of view, the division of the zodiac would be independent of the cardinal points of the solar cycle; the Hindu astrologers simply refer, in their division of the celestial regions, to a certain cyclic date which is marked by the coincidence of the twelve constellations with the twelve synonymous zodiacal signs, and they operate in this in an analogous manner to that which relates all the planetary movements effectuated during the course of an individual life, to the initial position of the sky at the moment of birth. On the other hand, the point of the view of the Hindu astrology corresponds well to the 'mythological' tendency of the Hindu civilisation whereas the Arab astrology is characterised by its deductive spirit; we want to say that the Hindus have spontaneously the tendency

In fact, the principle of distinction which measures the celestial space is essentially solar; it is by the revolution of the Sun that the qualitative differentiations of the directions, which radiate invariably from the terrestrial and human centre and which define the regions of the vault of the limit-sky, are operated. The solar cycle is therefore the direct expression of the Divine Act which puts the chaos in order. On the other hand, the sphere of the fixed stars – the innumerable multitude of which is like an image of so many luminous sources isolated in the shadows, and susceptible to entering into mutual relationships not yet manifested – symbolises, in relation to the zodiacal sphere, the cosmic potentiality which could never be exhausted and which avoids all intelligible definitions. – Thus we cannot distinguish the particular qualities of the sphere of the fixed stars, of which we nevertheless see traces, whereas we do know the qualities of the sphere without stars, which we do not see. In this there is a profound significance : we can in fact know the devolution of the world in principle, but we do not know all the 'material' potentialities that this devolution will wear out.

*　　*　　*

The extreme cycle which is manifested by the precession of the equinoxes, but of which we cannot determine the phases, should influence the totality of the sky by a successive predominance of certain cosmic or Divine Qualities. And since this major cycle is like the model of all the other cycles which are subordinated to it, one can attribute to it, by symbolic transposition, the contents or partitions analogous to those of an inferior cycle. Thus the *Sheikh al-akbar* attributes to the major cosmic cycle the determinations which he designates by the names of zodiacal signs and which follow each other in the

to 'divide' phenomena, so as to dissolve them in the consent of the Infinite, whereas the spirit of Islam which determines the Arab astrology deduces all from the idea of the Divine Unity. – As for the date of the coincidence of the two zodiacs, which is situated at about 400 A.D. it necessarily has to correspond to a 'renaissance' of astrological symbolism itself.

order of the annual movement of the Sun; which shows very well that it has nothing at all to do with the displacement of the vernal point in the constellations, a displacement which moves inversely to the solar movement. On the other hand, the Master assigns to the 'reigns' of these major 'signs', durations successively decreasing: Aries reigns for 12,000 years, Taurus for 11,000 years, Gemini for 10,000 years, and their durations decrease thus until the sign of Pisces whose reign numbers only 1,000 years. This decreasing also proves that it cannot be caused by spatial determinations like those which divide the zodiac, but that the zodiacal divisions are here transposed, due to a spiritual analogy, to determinations purely temporal, of a cycle the sub-division of which escapes from the spatial measure; in fact all spatial cycle is symmetrically divided, whereas a purely temporal cycle is divided in consequence of the progressive contraction of time.[5]

As to the effective duration of the different 'reigns' of these major 'signs', perhaps one should not see in the numbers of years indicated by Ibn 'Arabi anything other than purely symbolic numbers. All the same, the sum of all these 'reigns' is equal to the duration of three complete precessions of the equinoxes; – one should always take into account the fact that we can measure the complete duration of a precession (given that we can determine its speed), without being able to fix its terms in space. – If one refers to the Hindu theory of the cosmic cycles and if one counts for the first *yuga* of the actual *manvantara* the duration of one complete precession, the *manvantara*, being composed of four decreasing *yugas* according to the proportion 4 : 3 : 2 : 1, ought to contain 65,000 years, which differs by a half precession from the sum of 78,000 years which is deduced from the symbolism indicated by Ibn 'Arabi. We must add that the *Sheikh al-akbar* incidentally notes that the first 'sign' which reigned on the world was Libra, and that this was again domin-

[5] cf. The chapter 'Le temps changé en espace' in: *Le règne de la quantité et les signes des temps* of René Guénon.

ating in the era of the prophet Mohammed.[6] – We will willingly leave to others the task of conciliating these different factors. By the consideration of the precession of the equinoxes we are necessarily touching upon the limits of the cosmic whole which are characterised by the coincidence of the temporal and spatial determinations in the movement of the stars. This whole cannot be a closed system, and as soon as we consider its limits, we are short of measure, because time is measured by movement in space. The visible world is like a perfectly coherent figure, woven on a sliding base which escapes our hold.

Finally, we shall recall a formula of Muhyiddin Ibn 'Arabi that we have already cited incidentally during the course of our exposition, the cosmological and metaphysical importance of which is altogether fundamental: 'The world consists of the Unity of the Unified, whereas the Divine Independence resides in the Unity of the Unique'.

---

[6] We must point out that the sign of Libra does not exist in the most ancient representations of the zodiac. On the other hand, the ancient Chinese used to give the name Libra to the polar plough.

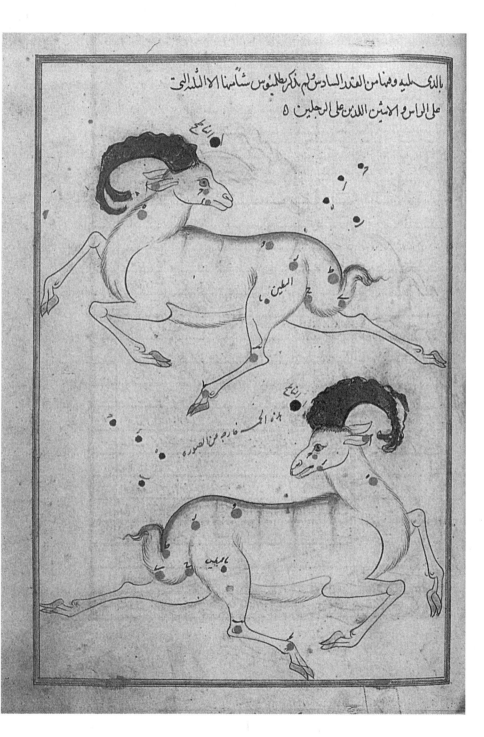

بالذي عليه وهنا من العقد السادس ولم يذكر بطليوس شأنها الا الثلثة التي
على الرأس و الاثنين اللذين على الرجلين ٥

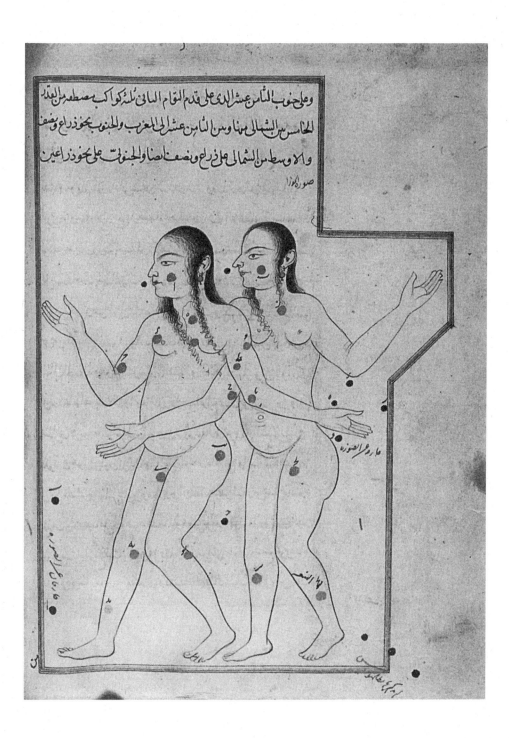

وعلى جنوب الثامن عشر الذي على قدم القائم الثاني ثلثة كواكب مصطفة من العقد
الخامس الشمالي منها ومن الثامن عشر الى المغرب والجنوب بنحو ذراع ونصف
والاوسط من الشمالي على ذراع ونصف اضعاف الجنوبي على نحو ذراعين
صورة الجوزاء

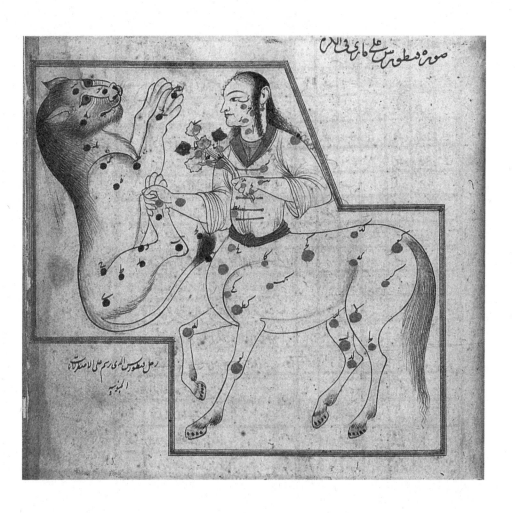